Makers of Empty Dreams

Also by Ian Seed

Anonymous Intruder (Shearsman Books, 2009)
Shifting Registers (Shearsman Books, 2011)

Chapbooks

No One Else at Home
        (translated from the Polish of Joanna Skalska) (Flax, 2007)
the straw which comes apart
        (translated from the Italian of Ivano Fermini) (Oystercatcher Press, 2010)
Amore mio (Flaxebooks, 2010)
Threadbare Fables (Like This Press, 2012)
Sleeping with the Ice Cream Vendor (Knives, Forks and Spoons Press, 2012)

Ian Seed

Makers
of
Empty
Dreams

Shearsman Books

First published in the United Kingdom in 2014 by
Shearsman Books
50 Westons Hill Drive
Emersons Green
BRISTOL
BS16 7DF

Shearsman Books Ltd Registered Office
30–31 St. James Place, Mangotsfield, Bristol BS16 9JB
(this address not for correspondence)

www.shearsman.com

ISBN 978-1-84861-345-4

Contents

'Whether this is the only way, or even the right way at all, can be decided only after one has gone along it.'
—Martin Heidegger

'Or, comme je regardais, je vis que ce que j'avais pris pour une mendiante c'était une caisse de bois peinte en vert qui contenait de la terre rouge et quelques bananes à demi pourries.'
—Max Jacob

I

City

I lived in Milan. I hadn't had sex for ages, yet one morning I noticed a rash of warts on my penis. I cycled as fast as I could to a doctor's surgery near the city centre. He told me it was nothing to worry about and gave me some cream in a tube with no label. When I came out, I saw a group of gypsy children clustered around my bike on the other side of the street. As I got closer, I realised it was a different bike. Mine had disappeared. 'Someone has stolen it,' I said. One boy raised a large spanner in the air, ready to hit me if I came any nearer. I walked away, thinking that if only I knew how to tell someone my story, I wouldn't feel so lonely.

Still Life

When I walk alone in the park among smiling families, larking youths and giggling girls, it's as beautiful as a painting come to life. It's as if someone were watching all of us. But what will happen when the gallery closes at the end of the day, and the bright picture is plunged into darkness? Will we still be here then? As I walk on, I feel strangers fix their gaze upon me, pinning me in the air. In the end, I am no longer moving at all, though I swing my arms and pump my legs absurdly like a puppet.

Town Centre

A thin youth with tousled hair and a wispy beard was walking from car to car stuck in the traffic. He tapped on each window and held out his hand for money. One driver, perhaps to show off in front of the woman next to him, jumped out of his car. Shouting and shaking his fist, he ran after the beggar all the way up the crowded high street. I thought he would catch him, but the beggar, turning a corner, ducked unseen into an Italian restaurant. I found him sitting at a table there, looking at a menu. The tablecloth was piled high with coins he'd taken from his pockets. He invited me to join him.

Autobiography

I found my friend Dante living in a small tent which he had set up just outside the railway station. No one objected to him being there, even though his tent was quite an obstruction during the rush hour. Yet there was no need for him to camp anywhere—he had over half a million pounds in the bank, most of which he'd earned from a self-published autobiography. He kept a copy of this by his side. It was well-thumbed and its pages were spotted with old stains. He would show it to anyone who dropped him a coin.

Ice-Cream Parlour

I have never seen so many different colours. The fat lady behind the counter smiles at my astonishment. This shop has been here for over three hundred years, she tells me. Her ice cream is made according to an ancient Italian recipe. Some say it even has the power to heal old wounds. I'm not sure I can trust her. Yet it would be discourteous of me not to buy an ice cream. I dig into my pockets. The lady keeps smiling at me.

Intimidation

The jackets in the second-hand clothes shop by the sea are much too dear. Yet the shopkeeper—a white-haired man with watery eyes behind rimless spectacles—will be offended if you don't try one on. He will pick one out for you from an overstuffed rail. You find that the jacket never fits, but he will give the sleeves a soft tug to make them longer or the shoulders a gentle punch to make them narrower. He will lightly stroke the jacket with his fingertips and tell you how wealthy its late owner was. When you look at yourself in the tilting mirror, he may even kiss you on the face to seduce or scare you into buying it.

Sale

We stand in a row, ready to greet the jostling crowd of customers outside the glass doors. There's a brand new product on offer: a glowing white tube, completely odourless and just a little bigger than a large thumb. It has multiple uses, including torch, mobile phone, and sex toy. We smile as we are meant to, yet there is a whiff of sour sweat—we know we are once again the makers of empty dreams. When the store finally opens, the crowd piles in. An elbow bashes my cheek. I'm scared of falling and being trampled on. At the same time, the warmth from all those bodies pressing against mine makes me come alive.

Chances

I wasn't sure which station was mine. In my broken Italian, I asked an old man who was standing next to me. It was a good twenty minutes yet, he said, swaying with the motion of the train. He began speaking to me in a mixture of English and Italian, telling me all about Milan. By the time I arrived at my stop, I found myself not wanting to leave him. Now I would have to find my own way through the streets of a city I had never seen before.

A few days later, I stumbled across the old man again in a market place. He grabbed my arm affectionately and invited me back to his house. The woman who opened the door was much younger than him. He introduced her as his wife. I remembered then that I had seen her the day before in the same market place, and had even exchanged flirtatious glances with her.

That evening I put on a fresh shirt and went for a stroll along the city's elegant boulevards. The people sitting at pavement tables regarded me with curiosity. I went into a café, sat down and ordered a carafe of wine. When it was time to ask for the bill, I realised I had left my wallet at the old man's house. I was embarrassed, but not as much as the waiter, whose main concern was to spare my feelings.

Marriage

He was much older than she was. One day, after a fall from a ladder, he was confined to bed for several weeks. He gave me a call and asked if I could help his wife move their new fridge.

As she and I pushed the fridge into place, her breast pressed into my arm. There in the kitchen, we had sex. She insisted on all kinds of positions, as if to take revenge for the immobility of her husband.

The Girl from Naples

I feel she will stop me floating away. She walks about the room in her floral dressing gown, picking up clothes from where we dropped them last night. The dressing gown makes her look much older than her twenty six years. An English girl wouldn't be seen dead in it. Neither would a girl from Milan. But Nunzia is from Naples, or somewhere near there. Her movements are heavy, solid, peasant-like. It must have been this which drew me to her in the first place, gave me a sense of security. In truth she is lost in Milan, as much a foreigner as I am. My little one, she calls me, though I am a good foot taller than she is. She comes back to bed with coffee on a tray for both of us. The bed sinks as she gets in beside me.

Estate

At that time I was working on a large estate, looking after the animals there. One little creature, a bit like an ugly guinea pig, would come and lie with me in bed to keep warm at nights. How clever, I thought, just like a family cat.

Each morning, a record was put onto an ancient turntable. All the employees were supposed to learn the song off by heart to perform at the annual fair. But the record was scratched and the needle kept jumping. Everyone complained that they would never be able to sing it properly. I couldn't see what all the fuss was about—it was easy to guess the missing bits. But I went along with the others, and in the end even came to believe the complaint myself.

When spring came, I would go for walks at dusk along the ridge overlooking the estate. My creature would accompany me. By this time he had grown as big and beautiful as a lion. I kept my relationship with him a secret. Otherwise they might persuade me he was too dangerous to sleep with.

Youth

Three beautiful Italian sisters lived next door. They were triplets, and all three were in love with me. Everyone said how lucky I was, but when their father demanded I make a proposal of marriage, I didn't know who to choose. For even when I made love to one of them, even when I held her gaze and our bodies trembled together, I never knew which of the three I was with.

Needs

I rented a room in an old house owned by an Italian family. They treated me like one of their own. Because one of the daughters was blind, none of the local men would consider her. Her father asked me if I would marry her. He gave me some pretty pebbles she had collected.

I put the pebbles into my pocket and took a stroll into town to think the matter over. On a street corner was a blind beggar. He wanted to know what the clinking sound was. I placed one of the pebbles in his palm. Caressing it, he asked if he could have the rest of them. That way, the sound of the pebbles rubbing together at night would keep him company when he slept on the street.

Sincerity

My youngest daughter was blinded in an accident. People often comment on how beautiful she is, but they avoid looking into her eye sockets when they say this.

Chrysalis

The creature came out from behind a dusty curtain. It was dirty and bleeding. We had thought it died years before when it shed its skin and became our beautiful daughter. Somehow it had survived. But what could we do with it now? We already had a daughter. And how could we tell her that she was this creature, too?

Poet's Pipe

In an old tobacconist's shop, I stumbled across a curved clay pipe, like the one smoked by the Italian poet, Cesare Pavese. I couldn't resist buying it. My Italian friends, who were all left-wingers and admirers of Pavese, were impressed when I took the pipe out of my jacket pocket, lit it, and puffed away as if I'd been smoking a pipe all my life.

The next day I was with my friends in a packed car driving down Via Roma in Turin. At the corner of a square we stopped outside a bar frequented by neo-fascists. My friends asked me to light my pipe. That would impress the fascists. They would realise that the lefties had a long-haired Englishman on their side.

I couldn't find my matches. However, as I puffed on the pipe and pretended to smoke it, a glow appeared. Somehow an ember had stayed alight from before.

One of my friends jumped out of the car and went into the bar. He pointed at me smoking my clay pipe. Soon the fascists and lefties were all pointing at me, and they were all laughing together.

Exchange

For a couple of years, I worked as a data administrator for a company in Milan. After the first year I still hadn't made any friends, and I would spend my evenings wandering the streets around the city centre. One evening I bumped into an ex-student from the time I was teaching English. Nunzia was someone I would make any excuse to get away from. She had bad breath, always leant too close to me and would never stop talking. But now I was happy to prolong the conversation for as long as I could, even to kiss her, if she'd let me, bad breath or no.

Trattoria

The owner tells me there is only one dish left on the menu tonight. He brings me a saucepan, lifts off the lid and shows me the unappetising remains of a meat soup. I tell him it looks delicious. Over the years he has become a kind of father to me, even though our relationship exists purely in the context of me coming to his trattoria nearly every evening. On those rare occasions when the place is full, he makes sure I have a table in a corner somewhere. Often, like tonight, I am the only person eating here. At times like this, I give his life its meaning.

The Excuse

I walked home from work along the misty river bank, where I knew there would be no one to disturb my thoughts. Earlier that day, my boss had taken me to one side and told me I had only one last chance. He wanted to see if I was 'serious' about my work. He was going to put me on a project run by a girl called Griffith. By coincidence this was a girl I had slept with a couple of weeks before.

I got back to my ground-floor flat with a feeling that I must escape from this foreign town where I had lived for years. But I had lost touch with everyone I knew back home.

Half-undressed, I lay down on my z-bed. I was just drifting off to sleep when I heard the voices of youths outside the window. Then there were footsteps coming down the hallway of the building. Looking through the peephole in my door, I saw a girl with straight dark hair cut all the same length to her jaw line. It was Griffith.

Still in my shirt and underpants, I opened the door and put my arms around her. I remembered that I hadn't got in touch with her since we had slept together. Perhaps that was why she looked so upset as she pulled away from me. But no. Standing in the middle of the room, she told me that my boss had said I was now a persona non grata in the department.

It really was time to leave.

'Griffith,' I said, raising my hand.

She waited for me to speak, but I wasn't sure anymore what it was I wanted to say. In the silence that followed, I realised the youths had also stopped talking. I had the impression that they were listening at the window, but I didn't want to open the curtains to find out, not in front of Griffith, who was breathing heavily, staring at me with those dark liquid eyes of hers, the ones I found so irresistible.

Accident

The baby fell from the balcony just as I was walking past. Luckily I was fast enough to catch it. The mother didn't seem at all grateful. But I said nothing when I handed the baby back to her because I recognised her as the woman whom I met for sex on an almost daily basis in another part of town.

Nightclub

I didn't remember who she was, but when I began kissing her, I knew from the feel of her lips that she was someone I had once kissed years before.

Thirst

My girlfriend and I were thirsty after walking for hours in Paris. We went into a bar, only to find it empty, but at the back there was a tiny garden with an apple tree. I wasn't sure if the apples were ripe, but my girlfriend picked one and told me it was the sweetest she'd ever tasted.

A burly man came rushing towards us.

'This is my bar! How dare you steal from me!'

'It's just an apple growing on a tree,' I said.

He clenched his fists and took a step closer.

I took my girlfriend's hand and led her away. We walked along the street, taking it in turns to bite the apple.

Bad Faith (1)

It was always the same homeless old woman outside the metro entrance.

One day, instead of simply dropping a coin into the filthy handkerchief by her side, I asked: 'Whatever happened to you?'

'I was a collaborator during the war,' she murmured. 'Now, no one will give me work or shelter.'

'But that was forty years ago,' I said.

I raised my voice and tried to catch the eyes of the passers by. 'Lots of people, even your great Jean Paul Sartre, slept with the enemy in one way or another.'

But this only made everyone pass by all the faster.

2

At the New Airport

There was a steep slide for passengers instead of an escalator to speed things up. I was looking forward to trying it out. However, something had gone wrong at the check-in. There was no-one behind the desk. When a woman finally arrived in a blood-red uniform, I recognised her as someone I'd once had an affair with. I was tempted to use my connection to jump the queue. The idea of missing the plane seemed unbearable. I would have to take the train all the way back up north with my heavy suitcase. I would arrive home weeping, and my wife and children would weep with me.

Investment

I was sent to work on a business project in China. On the underground train you could buy a carnet of ten tickets from a lady who walked through the carriages with a glass box hanging from a cord around her neck. All you had to do was put some coins into a slot at the top of the box. It looked heavy and the ticket lady was tiny, but she kept smiling. There was another slot on the side of the box, into which you could insert bank notes to invest on the Chinese stock exchange. If by the end of the train journey, the stocks had gone up, the lady would give you your winnings. One morning I made over a thousand pounds in just a few minutes. Now I could phone my wife back home with good news. I was worth something.

Creatures

There was a mottled snake which made its home under our kitchen sink. If it was venomous, I would have to kill it. Otherwise, we could keep it as a pet.

There was a woman upstairs with smoothest skin who lay naked in her bed at nights, but I wasn't sure it was me she was waiting for.

Around the corner was a small store no one went to anymore. I felt I must go there soon. I would buy a bottle of wine and chat to the Indian owner the way I used to. But first I had to decide upon the snake and the woman.

Prize-Giving

The poet P. resents having to travel with me to Italy for the ceremony. He is a full-time professional while I have only just published my first collection. In the airport lounge, he takes out his laptop, puts his headphones on and stares at the screen while I drink my coffee. He only comes to life when one of his female students appears from nowhere. Tearing off the headphones, he picks her up and twirls her around. She is half his age, the same age as my daughter, who yesterday while we were out walking in a nature reserve approached a stag with enormous horns. The stag did not move away, but stared at her with friendly curiosity. It was only when I came near him that he turned and fled.

The Poet's Day

The young Italian teacher who works in the school where I am running a workshop, is a little flirtatious with me. 'You should smile more,' she tells me. After all, she is able to smile though she has a terrible toothache. 'Everything will turn out for the best,' she says.

At lunchtime we look for a spot in the grass where we can redraft our poems. There is one place where the grass has been all smoothed down. This will do, I think, but the others want to find somewhere where the grass is fresher.

When I return to the university in the afternoon to give my report, the poet P. tells me in front of the students that I should be writing fiction for children rather than my risqué poetry. 'But my poems use the senses to inhabit meaning,' I say. He turns to the students and shrugs: 'Who is going to tell him the truth he doesn't want to hear?'

Alba

My wife and I walked among the well-dressed Italians, feeling shabby and foreign. We were looking for the house where Cesare Pavese once lived. I had seen a black-and-white photo of it. I knew it was somewhere near the main square, under some arches. We stopped to ask one or two passers-by, but they shrugged us away. My wife said she was tired. This was my pilgrimage after all, not hers. We agreed to meet later back at the hotel. As soon as she was gone, a woman pressed against me in the crowd. She whispered in my ear that she knew of a room where she and I could make love. But would I remember how to kiss a stranger?

After the Business Meeting

I spoke in Italian to the waitress at the Hotel Savona. The young salesman I was dining with seemed impressed. As we ate, he listened to my stories of deals I had made or blown over the years as if I were the greatest of raconteurs. But when he made some feeble excuse and left halfway through the meal, I realised he had only spent time in my company to see if he could make use of me. I lit a cigarette and watched the smoke blow over the remains of the meal on his plate. After a while, the waitress approached with two cups of coffee. I wondered what would happen if I invited her to sit down with me and drink the unwanted coffee.

Return

When I returned to the Italian town where I'd lived as a young man, there was no longer any one there that I recognised. In the evening, I went to the trattoria where I used to eat, but now it was run by a different family. Having drunk too much wine and grappa, I got lost in the maze of streets and alleys that I'd known so well. Turning a corner, I tripped on a large cobblestone. A passing youth pulled me to my feet. With his untidy hair and beard, and his oversized coat on a skinny frame, he reminded me of a partisan. He stared at me with a questioning look, as if to ask what an old foreigner was doing, wandering around these streets at this time of night. When I thanked him for his help, he replied in what I thought was some kind of dialect. But as he went on, I realised it was just that I could no longer understand the language I thought I'd never forget.

Authenticity

I was the only foreigner to attend the commemoration. I walked up the steep hill to Valdivilla, a village where Italian Resistance fighters had been killed in their last defeat at the hands of the fascists. It was rainy, muddy and slippery—much as it had been on that day in February 1945.

Later, driving back to the airport past run-down estates and fast-food joints, I became afraid that I would die among these, unnoticed.

Fair

I was already dead, standing on the side of a bare windy hill. After a while, people from the village below began to arrive and put up tents for a fair. They had no idea that a dead person was among them. However, I must have been visible, for every now and then one of them would turn towards me with an inquisitive glance, as if to ask what a stranger was doing there before the fair was ready.

Academic

Turning the corridor I bumped into someone I hadn't seen for years. It was Mr T., my old 'A' level history teacher. He must have moved to the university where I was now also teaching.

'Well, hello there! How are you?' I said, wanting to tell him the news of my PhD on Pavese and to show him that I was a teacher too now, no longer the obnoxious teenager I once had been.

He stared at me before replying, obviously trying to place my face.

'Things aren't too good, I'm afraid. My mother died a week ago. I've only just come back to work.' He turned his eyes aside with a mixture of sorrow and irritation. 'I must go.'

When he pushed open the door onto the stairwell, I thought for a moment he was going to throw himself over the banister.

I realised that not only had he not recognised me, but that he could not possibly have been Mr T, who would be in his eighties or already dead. This was a man much younger than me.

Old Haunt

Back in Milan, I go in search of the English bookshop that I used to love visiting years ago, a little way off from the city centre. It takes me a while now to find it. Inside, instead of the wooden staircase up to the next floor, there is a shiny escalator. At the top of the escalator, instead of the ramshackle rows of second-hand books that I used to spend hours browsing, there are glass shelves with glossy magazines. There is even a hamburger stand where the 'Beat Poets' section used to be, though at least the stand is fashioned in 1950s style.

In the Anniversary TV Special, the Real

Elvis never appears. It's just a series of impersonators, who sing and dance in a competition for Best Elvis. My grandmother stares at the screen. She has such a short memory now she thinks each of the impersonators is Elvis. But then they all look alike with their greased up hair, fake tan and white jumpsuits. And I've heard that the Real Elvis is somewhere still alive, that he even sings on these shows, but never wins.

In the Empty Church

There was Elvis alone, singing from music sheets laid out on the stone floor. I wondered how he had forgotten those gospel songs he had sung all his life. He was so entranced by the act of singing that he didn't notice me standing there. He was of course much older than when he died, yet his voice was more powerful than it had ever been. I wondered if the ghost of my father could see him too – I was sure he would be impressed.

A Life

When I woke up, it had gone from winter to summer. I stepped outside into a meadow full of bright butterflies and hopping rabbits. I realised it was just a cartoon world, but I didn't know how to return to my own.

Over the hill was a pretty shepherd girl and an old man with a white beard. They nodded absurdly at me. I am not like you, I thought, I am real.

I came to the sea, but since it was a cartoon sea, would I get wet if I stepped into it? I was afraid to try, but here was a mermaid inviting me in. If I held her hand, would I feel it in mine? If she wanted to make love, what would I do?

Textures

Emptiness is not nothing
　　—Martin Heidegger

Touching one hand with the other, you remember how it is to touch and be touched: your body finds its place once again in the arrangements of a landscape whose colours and smells are formed inside your heart. If one evening you remember how on another evening you took her hand in yours, then it will always be true that you remembered—though the picture exists only for as long as you can see it, or hold her in your empty arms.

Recruit

As I walked by the army recruitment office to go to the pub where I sometimes sit alone over a pint, a youth, who was pissing in a high arc against the wall, turned to see who was passing by behind him. His piss splashed my thigh. I wondered if I could still go into the pub. Would anyone be able to smell it? Laughing, he said he was sorry, that he was just practising for being in the army. He held onto one leg and hopped around on the other. He said he was practising for being wounded.

Bad Faith (2)

I was in the war like everyone else. But was I? The other soldiers kept testing my commitment with new tricks. One night a woman with scarred skin came to my bed. She pressed herself against me and asked if I found her beautiful. I whispered that I did. She had two children, she told me, did I still find her beautiful?

In the morning, the other soldiers wanted to know if I would marry her. When I said that I would, one of them laughed and pointed to the ring I was already wearing. They threw hundreds of pebbles at my face. The pebbles grew brightly-coloured wings and flew around me. I could have spent a lifetime watching them, but there was a war on.

3

Personal History

My wife and I are back in Warsaw. I have no job. How will I justify my existence to her family? What's almost as bad is that I have forgotten how to speak Polish. Funnily enough, my mother-in-law now speaks English. She even mentions that she has been able to read an old book of poems of mine. She says with approval mixed with regret that if only I'd stuck to my poetry earlier on in life, I might have made something of myself!

When I ask where she has learnt English, she tells me of a young English teacher who has recently arrived in Poland. He is really nice, keen to learn all about the Polish culture and language, not like most of the stuck-up Brits who come for a year and disappear to go onto better things, sometimes picking up a Polish wife on the way.

At that moment, the young teacher arrives at the door. I can see why my mother-in-law is so charmed by him. He has such a disarming smile and such sincere interest in his soft brown eyes. He chats to me as if I were a young man like himself. I take up his invitation to go for a 'lads' drink' with him in town.

Walking through the city centre, we meet two girls that he knows. A few years ago I would have shown off my Polish, but now I say nothing. After a drink in a bar, we all go to the cinema and huddle close together on our seats in the back row, like naughty school children. While the two girls nip off to the toilet, he tells me that I can have my pick of either one of them: they both like me because I have not made a pass at them as Brits usually do. 'But I'm a married man!' I say. 'A father with responsibilities.' He looks at me as if only now realising how old I am.

The next day, early in the morning, I am walking along the Vistula river. Polish military airplanes are performing exercises, flying incredibly low, just above the river's surface. They seem to swerve a little towards my side of the river as they pass. I try to catch a glimpse of the pilots' faces, but they are moving too fast. Yet they must be able to see me, and they must be thinking how foolish I am to be walking all alone so early in the day. Or perhaps they are disappointed because I am the only audience they have.

But now here is that young man, coming in the opposite direction. Soon our paths will cross again.

The Test

My wife and I were put up in a posh hotel for the languages conference. It had been arranged that she would spend the first evening with a handsome Italian, while I would take an Italian woman out to dinner. It was a kind of test for us: did we still have the power to seduce? If we did, would we remain faithful to each other?

While I was having a bath, I noticed a turd floating around in the water. Where had it come from? There was a knock on the bathroom door. I thought it would be my wife, but it was my date already waiting for me, and wanting to come in.

A Knock at the Door

While I'm in bed with my wife, a man arrives from the bank. There's a debt from years ago that she's forgotten to pay. The man resembles Nick Clegg, and he leers at her breasts. He says he knows what it's like to be in debt, being a politician. After I have thrown him out, my wife and I make love. But it's over quickly, and she won't look me in the eye.

Moral

I had a rash of warts on my foot. The Arab doctor called in his assistant, a boy of about thirteen. He spoke to him in Arabic and gave him a kind of scraping tool with a silver blade. The boy looked at me as if torn between his fear of hurting me and his desire to please his master. I closed my eyes and tried not to clench my fists.

When the boy applied the blade, I felt almost nothing, only a vague tickling. I wondered if I should tell the doctor about the much bigger warts on my belly and ribcage. There it might really hurt, for when I opened my eyes the doctor was staring at me as if I had not yet received the punishment I deserved.

Chance

He tells me of a trip to Denmark when he was twenty one. At an open-air concert in Copenhagen his hand brushed against the hand of a girl in the crowd. They stood without speaking in the sun, pretending to listen to the orchestra while their fingers locked together. When the music came to an end, ashamed of his stutter, he watched the girl walk away, his palm soaked in her sweat.

Now dying, my father wonders what might have happened if only he had dared speak to her. Perhaps she would be here with him now, holding his hand. As if he could have his life all over again.

A Gesture

When you discover the skeleton in the cupboard, what do you do with the bones? It's always too late – you're no longer the child stepping off a train, looking for a face at the end of the platform. You never reach the grey house at the end of the street: in the front room, the faint smell of your father's sweat, the book open where he dropped it, the yellowed keys of a piano neither of you learnt to play.

Distraction

Cows and sheep keep criss-crossing the lane. It's like strolling through a nineteenth-century landscape. But I can hear a car approaching much too fast. It screeches around the corner and crashes into the side of a cow's head. Yet the cow remains standing, with one half of its face all swollen.

The driver, a burly man, gets out to inspect his car for damage.

'We'd better tell the farmer,' I say.

He glowers at me. 'No, don't that. You'll only upset him.'

I say nothing, but that evening in the pub I tell the farmer what has happened. He begs me to help him catch the man: 'You go to one end of the lane and I'll go to the other. That way we'll cut him off.'

It's much too late for that, but I don't want to hurt the farmer's feelings. I am about to follow him out of the pub when a girl starts playing the piano. She plays so beautifully that I am rooted to the spot. It makes me wonder why I never learnt to play an instrument.

When the farmer returns empty-handed hours later, he seems puzzled rather than annoyed to find me still standing in the same place at the bar.

Attitude

It was a sweltering day. I'd walked several miles through baking fields when I came across a farmhouse with a large tap sticking out of its wall. Above the tap was a sign: 'Footpath walkers welcome to use'. A lad of about eight years old was filling up a tin tankard. Once the tankard was full, he poured the water away. I thought that perhaps he was rinsing his cup, but then he did the same thing all over again. I watched the rills of water run down the path and fill the cracks in the dry mud. This game went on for so long that I thought I would faint from thirst. I wanted to tell the boy to stop messing around. But he seemed so sure of himself that I assumed he was the farmer's son, while I was no more than a passer-by.

Ghost

I met up with my father in a hotel lobby. He asked me about the briefcase with all the letters and papers inside that he had left with me years before. It was still safe, I assured him. I remembered that some of the letters were ones I had written to him in the neat handwriting one learns at school. The tears rose from the pit of my stomach. I couldn't stop them. My father frowned and went red. He was ashamed that his son, a middle-aged man, could cry in public like a child.

Holiday Camp

I am dancing with my wife and daughter, out in the open air. They are laughing at me because my mind is elsewhere. I leave the dance floor and walk through the pine wood to my mother's room in our holiday chalet. It has occurred to me that perhaps she is dying. I find her asleep. For the first time in my adult life, I hold her and tell her I love her. She wakes as I am doing so. She wonders what all the fuss is about.

Beside Me

In the Quaker Meeting House, the sudden presence of my
father, not as a ghost which cannot die because incomplete, but
as a breathing spirit—I see him sitting here sixty years ago in
this light-filled room, lost in his thoughts, and next to him my
mother, her hands clasped in her lap uncertainly, as they are now.

Travel

On my way to buy some euros, I bumped into my old friend Jeremy Over, the poet. He said he would keep me company for a while. In the bureau de change, there was no exchange rate displayed anywhere, and they seemed annoyed that I wanted to find out what it was. Moreover, the man behind the glass counter with his uniform and severe expression looked more like a German customs official than someone trying to please his customers. When I insisted he tell me the rate, he said 'three to four'. I took this to mean that three pounds would be worth four euros. When I asked if I was right, he made some sly reference to the philosopher Nietzsche, as if to show how ignorant I was. Having written my dissertation on Nietzsche many years before, I was able to retort with an apt quotation—'Better to live among ice than among European virtues'—before turning on my heel and walking out. I went in search of another bureau de change that I knew existed somewhere off the main street. After ten minutes, I still hadn't found it. 'I'm sure it's down this alleyway,' I said to Jeremy. But I could see now his patience was wearing thin and that it was time for us to part company.

The Philosopher

During the last months of Nietzsche's life, I stayed next to him in his bed. He lay in his nightshirt, propped up on great pillows, gazing into space. I didn't know if he knew I was there or not. Yet sometimes he would turn towards me with his dark tearful eyes.

'It's good, isn't it?' he said.

His sister Elizabeth would bring in tea for us both on a silver tray. 'This is the first time he has spoken in years,' she told me.

I was glad to be of use, but wished I'd known him before when he was writing his last books of philosophy in Turin: *Twilight of the Idols*, *The Anti-Christ*, and *Ecce Homo*.

My wife and daughter were not happy. After Nietzsche died, I found all their voice mails on my mobile. They had been trying to get in touch with me for a long time—without success, since there was no coverage where I was.

Exile

There's the path if you chuse it
—John Clare

I pursue him for years through spattered streets. One morning I
abandon the chase and take the road out of town. Puffs of cloud
keep pace with me. I am nothing, and alone, and everything
is possible. I walk until the air grows brown, weaving dreams
around trees. Their branches brush my face like fingers, or tear
as if their stories would draw blood.

Faith

The tower in the distance has finally pierced the sky. When we first heard it was being built, we thought we had found a real story with a happy ending. Like everyone else in this gaping crowd, we have grown old gossiping about where the tower might lead. We know now God was only a figure carved into the air by a dying hand. Our tears are sincere. We believe that this new story of loss is the true one of our lives.

Acknowledgements

My thanks to:

August 1st 2013 (Martin Stannard), *Dwang* (Michael Curran), *The Café Irreal* (G.S. Evans, Alice Whittenburg), *Free Verse* (Jon Thompson), *Harlequin* (Luke Smith, Paul Sweeten), *Kaffeeklatsch* (Joey Connolly, Matt Halliday, Stephen Nashef), *PN Review* (Michael Schmidt), *Sentence: A Journal of Prose Poetics* (Brian Johnson), *Tears in the Fence* (David Caddy), and *Tower of Babel* (Nikolai Duffy, Rupert M Loydell).

Lightning Source UK Ltd.
Milton Keynes UK
UKOW03f0858100614

233150UK00001B/207/P